Wonders

McGraw Hill Education

Cover and Title Page: Nathan Love

www.mheonline.com/readingwonders

Mc
Graw
Hill
Education

Send all inquiries to:
McGraw-Hill Education
2 Penn Plaza
New York, NY 10121

ISBN: 978-0-02-131249-8
MHID: 0-02-131249-4

Printed in the United States of America

11 LKV 25   D

Wonders

ELD
Companion Worktext

Program Authors

Diane August

Jana Echevarria

Josefina V. Tinajero

McGraw Graw Hill Education

Think it Through

The Big Idea

Think it Through

The Big Idea

How can a challenge bring out our best?

Stephen Simpson/Iconica/Getty Images

TALK ABOUT IT

 **Essential Question**

Where do good ideas come from?

>> *Go Digital*

4

What idea does the boy have to make a bike? Write the things the boy uses to make a bike in the idea web.

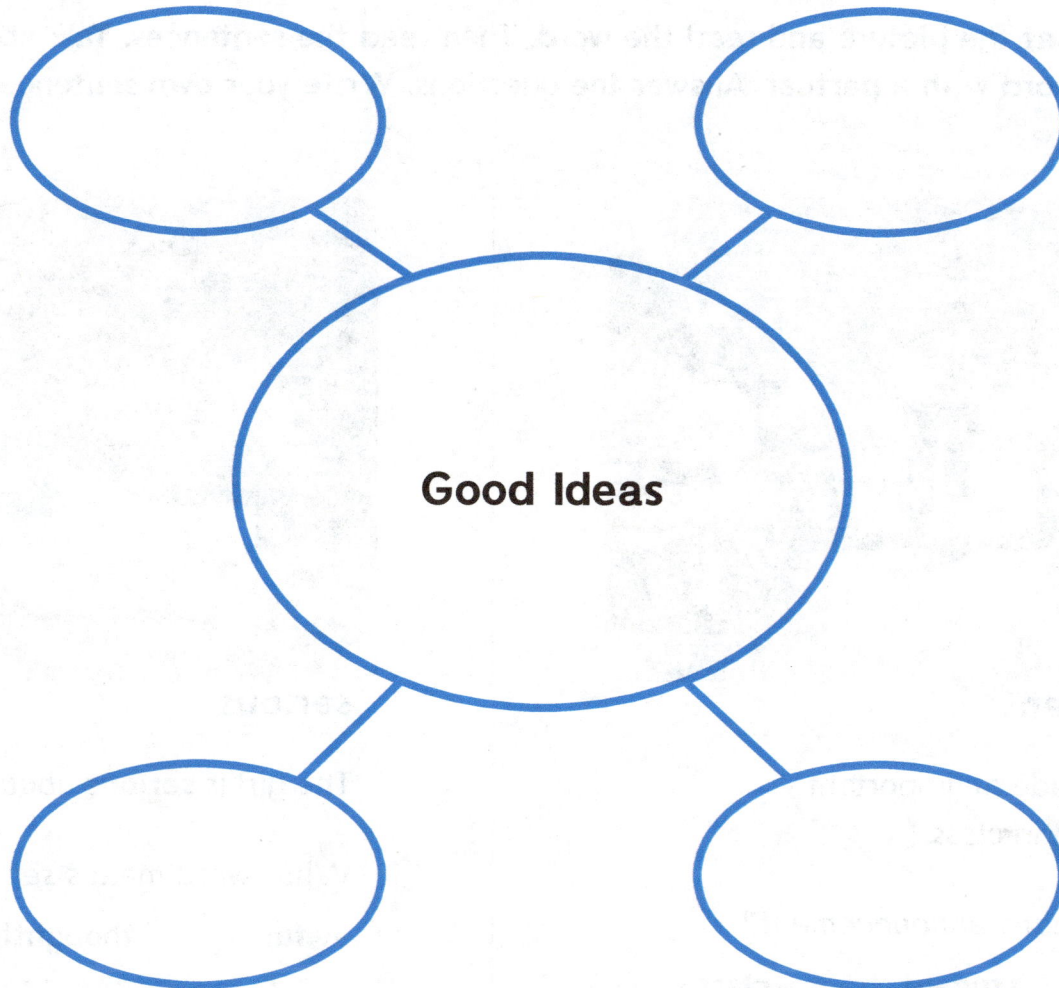

Good Ideas

Discuss how the boy gets his ideas to make a bike. Use the words from the chart. You can say:

The boy gets his ideas from _____ and _____.

COLLABORATE Look at the picture and read the word. Then read the sentences. Talk about the word with a partner. Answer the questions. Write your own sentence.

announcement

The student made an important **announcement** in class.

What word means *announcement?*

message   student   class

When do you hear an announcement?

I hear an announcement _____.

serious

The girl is **serious** about studying.

What word means *serious?*

awful   thoughtful   thankful

What are you serious about?

I am serious about _____.

Words and Phrases: *un-* and *-ly*

The prefix *un-* means "not."

unlucky = not lucky

Why are the people not lucky?

The people are **unlucky** because it is raining.

The suffix *-ly* tells how something is done.

kindly = in a kind way

What is the boy doing to be kind?

The boy is **kindly** helping another person.

COLLABORATE Talk with a partner. Look at the pictures. Read the sentences. Circle the meaning of the underlined word.

The dog is <u>unclean</u>.

not clean   **in a clean way**

The boy is playing <u>loudly</u>.

very loud   **not loud**

(t)Dennis MacDonald/Alamy; (tr)Design Pics Inc./Alamy; (bl)Julia Christe/fStop Images/Getty Images; (br)Fuse/Getty Images

COLLABORATE

1 Talk About It

Look at the picture. Read the title. Discuss what you see. Use these words.

dragon   big   problem

Write about what you see.

I see _____

_____ .

Why is the dragon a problem?

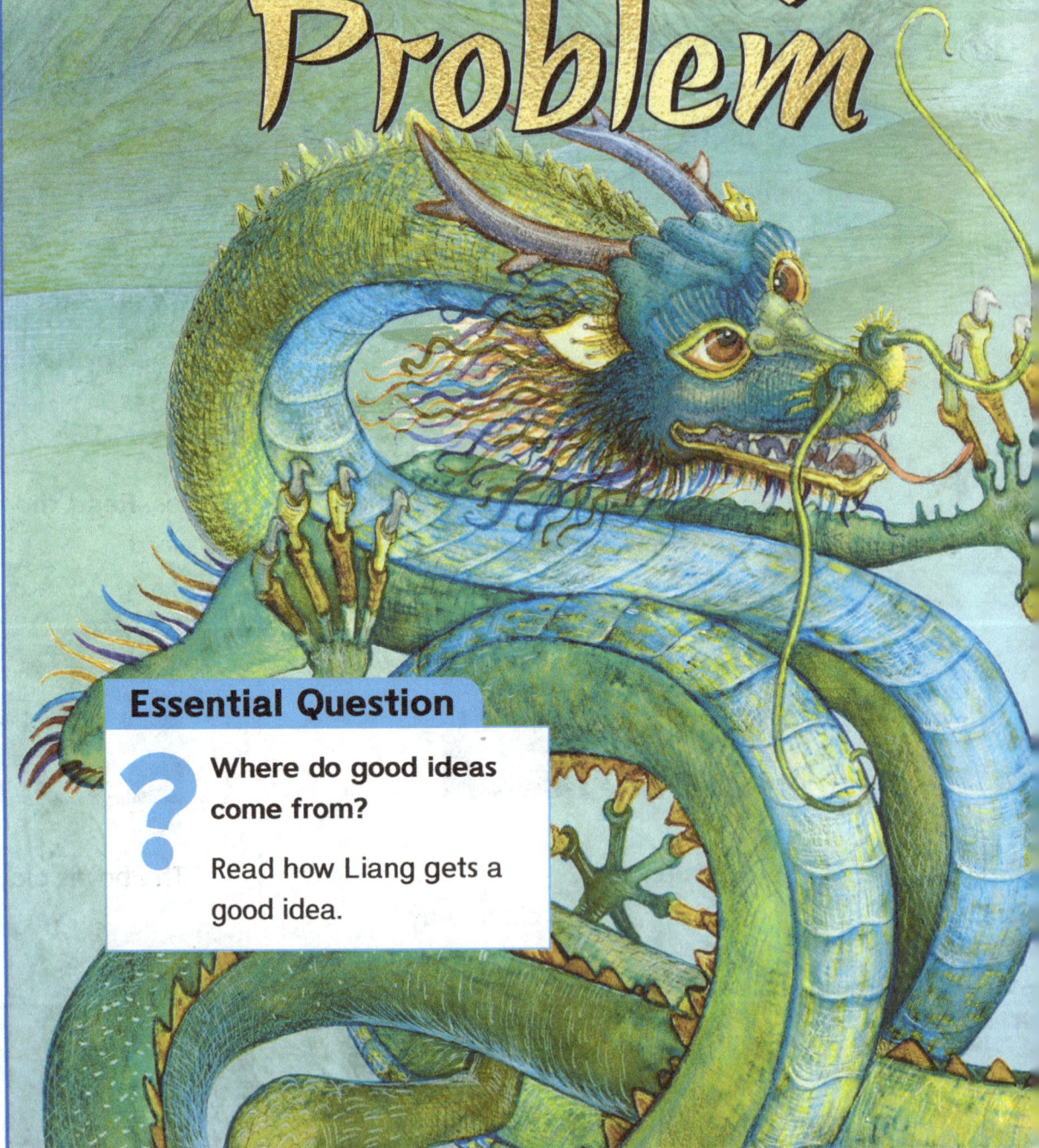

The dragon is a problem because

_____

_____

Take notes as you read the story.

The Dragon Problem

Essential Question

? **Where do good ideas come from?**

Read how Liang gets a good idea.

Once upon a time, there lived a young man named Liang. During the day Liang helped his father build wood tables. At night, Liang made original wood toys. He **carved** dragons with long tails and sharp claws.

Liang knew a lot about dragons because a big dragon lived on a mountain nearby. Sometimes the dragon flew down on the village. He ate cows, pigs, and any people unlucky to be around!

The Emperor had a summer home near the village, but he did not know how to get rid of the dragon.

One day, the Emperor and his family were going to their summer home. Liang watched them ride by. Princess Peng saw Liang and smiled kindly at him. Liang was in love!

That night Liang told his father he wanted to marry Princess Peng.

His father said, "You are joking!"

Liang said, "No, I am **serious**!"

His father laughed so hard he broke his chair.

Valerie Sokolova

1 Sentence Structure Ⓐ Ⓒ Ⓣ

Reread the third and fourth sentences in the first paragraph. Underline the word in the third sentence that can replace the pronoun *He* in the fourth sentence. Write the word in the sentence.

_____ carved dragons with long tails and sharp claws.

2 Specific Vocabulary Ⓐ Ⓒ Ⓣ

Reread the last sentence in the first paragraph. The word *carved* means "cut something hard into a shape." What did Liang carve to make dragons?

Liang carved _____.

3 Comprehension Sequence

What happened after Princess Peng smiled at Liang?

After Princess Peng smiled at Liang, he _____.

9

Text Evidence

1 Sentence Structure (A)(C)(T)

Reread the second paragraph. Circle the punctuation marks that show someone is speaking. Underline the person who is speaking.

COLLABORATE

2 Talk About It

Reread the sixth paragraph. Why is Ling Ling's idea a good idea?

Ling Ling's idea is a good idea

because _____

_____.

3 Comprehension

Sequence

Reread the last paragraph. What did Liang do when he went home?

First, Liang made _____.

Next, he pulled it _____.

Then, he set it _____.

Liang said quietly, "I will marry the Princess!"

The next morning, the emperor made an **announcement**: "The person who gets rid of the dragon will marry Princess Peng."

Liang was excited. He looked for his friend Lee. Liang wanted Lee to help him. But Lee was away. Liang was sad because he did not have any ideas.

Some children were playing nearby. They asked, "Liang, what is wrong?"

Liang said, "I need an idea to get rid of the dragon."

Ling Ling said, "I have an idea. You can carve a big dragon and leave it by the cave. It will scare the dragon away."

"Good idea!" Liang said. He ran home and worked frantically. Liang made a big, scary dragon. He pulled the wood dragon up the mountain in a cart. Liang set the dragon near the cave.

Liang hid behind a tree. He made a loud roar. The dragon ran out of the cave and said, "What's that noise?" Then he saw the big dragon. He shouted, "Go away, or I will eat you!"

But the wood dragon did not move. The dragon thought, "He must be very strong because he is not afraid of me." The dragon decided to take a long trip.

The dragon said, "I am leaving now. You can stay in my cave as long as you like." Then he flew away.

The next year, Liang and Princess Peng were married and lived happily ever after.

Make Connections

? Talk about where Liang's idea for scaring the dragon came from.
ESSENTIAL QUESTION

Tell about a time when a friend helped you think of a good idea.
TEXT TO SELF

Valerie Sokolova

1 Comprehension
Sequence

Reread the first paragraph. What happened after Liang roared? Underline the sentence that tells you.

2 Sentence Structure A C T

Reread the second sentence in the second paragraph. Why does the dragon think the wooden dragon is strong? Draw a box around the part of the sentence that tells you.

COLLABORATE

3 Talk About It

How did Liang's skill as a carver help him marry the princess?

Liang's skill as a carver helped

him because _____

_____

_____.

Respond to the Text

Partner Discussion Work with a partner. Read the questions about "The Dragon Problem." Show where you found text evidence. Write the page numbers. Then describe what you learned.

COLLABORATE

What did you learn about Liang?

Liang carves _____.

I read that Liang wants to marry _____.

In the text, Liang has to get rid of _____.

Text Evidence 🔍

Page(s): _____

Page(s): _____

Page(s): _____

How does Liang solve the dragon problem?

Liang wants to find Lee because _____.

I read that Liang gets an idea from _____.

In the text, Ling Ling's idea is to _____

_____.

Text Evidence 🔍

Page(s): _____

Page(s): _____

Page(s): _____

COLLABORATE

Group Discussion Present your answers to the class. Cite text evidence for your ideas. Listen to and discuss the group's opinions about your ideas.

I think your idea is _____.

Write Work with a partner. Look at your notes about "The Dragon Problem." Write your answer to the Essential Question. Use text evidence to support your answer. Use vocabulary words in your writing.

How does Liang get a good idea?

Liang wants to get rid of the dragon because _____

_____.

Ling Ling gives him the idea to _____

_____.

It was a good idea because _____

_____.

Share Writing Present your writing to the class. Then talk about their opinions. Think about their ideas. Explain why you agree or disagree with their ideas. You can say:

I agree with _____.

I do not agree because _____.

Write to Sources

Take Notes About the Text I took notes about the story on a chart to help answer the question: *What happens when Liang returns to the village after he scares the dragon?*

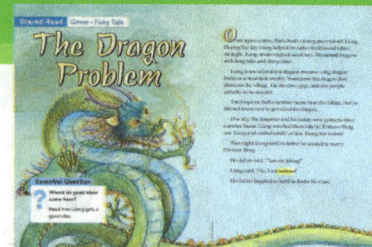

The Dragon Problem

pages 8–11

First, Liang falls in love with the princess.

↓

Then the Emperor says the person who gets rid of the dragon can marry the princess.

↓

Next, Ling Ling gives Liang a great idea.

↓

Later, Liang makes a giant wood dragon. It scares the real dragon away.

Write About the Text I used my notes from my sequence chart to write a paragraph to describe what happens after Liang scares the dragon away.

Student Model: *Narrative Text*

The wood dragon scares the real dragon away! Liang picks up green scales from the dragon to show everyone. He runs to the village. He tells Ling Ling her great idea worked. Then the children go with Liang to tell the Emperor the good news.

TALK ABOUT IT

COLLABORATE

Text Evidence

Draw a box around a sentence that comes from the notes. Does the sentence describe a detail?

Grammar

Circle a word that describes *scales*. Why did Kyle add this detail?

Connect Ideas

Underline the two sentences that tell what Liang does when he knows that the dragon is gone. How can you use the word *then* to show the order of events?

Your Turn

COLLABORATE

Add an event to the story. Tell what happens when Liang tells his father he is marrying the princess. Use details from the story.

>> *Go Digital*
Write your response online. Use your editing checklist.

? Essential Question
How do your actions affect others?

>> *Go Digital*

COLLABORATE What are the girls doing? Describe how their actions will make others feel. Write words in the chart.

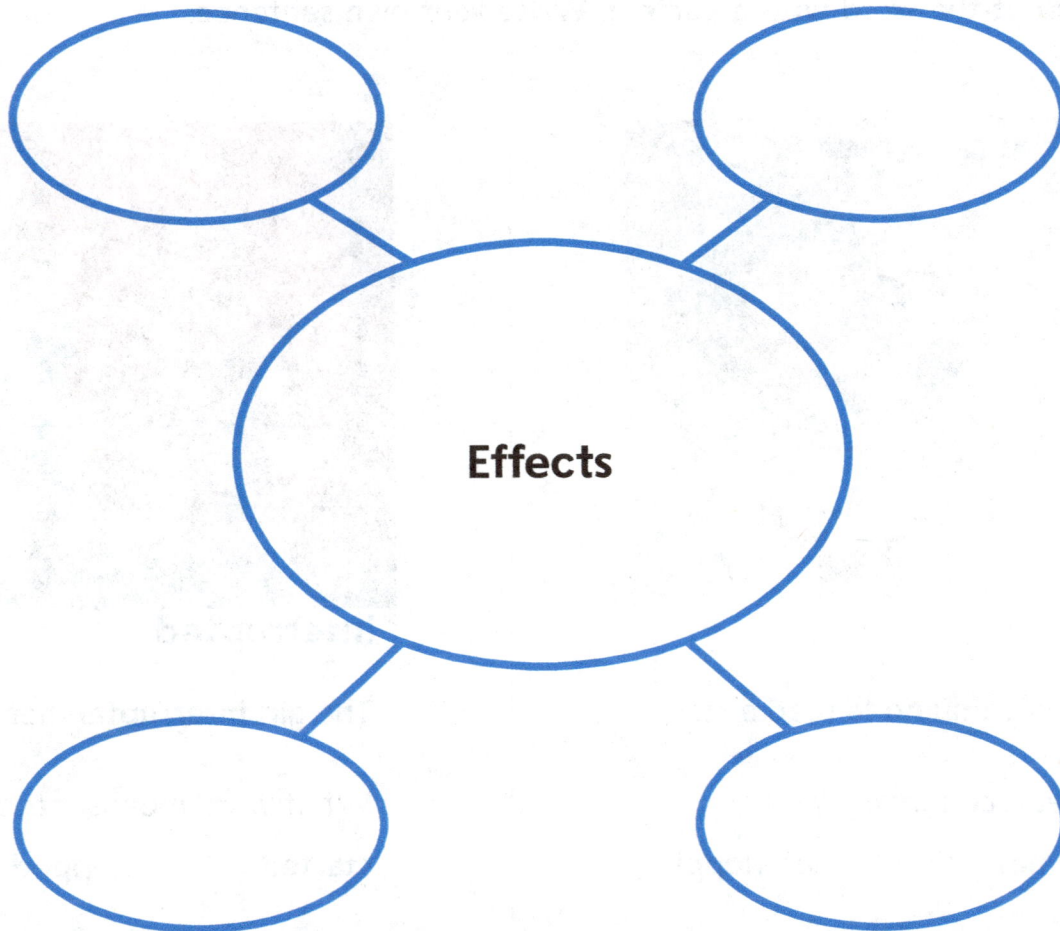

Effects

Discuss how the girls' actions can make others feel. Use the words from the chart. You can say:

The girls' actions can make others feel _____

and _____.

Masterfile

More Vocabulary

Look at the picture and read the word. Then read the sentences. Talk about the word with a partner. Write your own sentence.

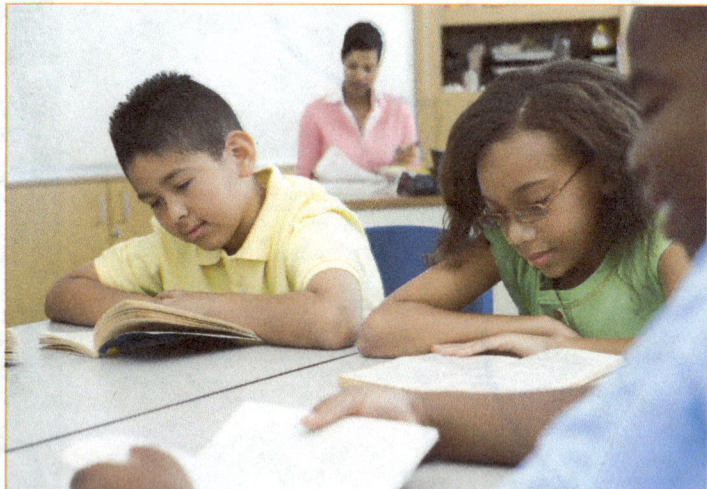

continuing

The children are **continuing** to read a story.

Which words mean *continuing*?

not walking   not going   not stopping

What books are you continuing to read?

I am continuing to read _____

_____.

interrupted

The girl **interrupted** her grandfather's nap.

What word means *interrupted*?

started   stopped   played

When have you been interrupted?

I have been interrupted _____

_____.

Words and Phrases: Homophones *to* and *too*

The word *to* means "toward."

Where are the children going?

The children are going **to** school.

The word *too* means "also."

Can I play with you?

I will play, **too**.

Talk with a partner. Look at the pictures. Read the sentences. Write the word that completes the sentence.

They go _____ the beach on the weekend.

to   too

These children go to the beach, _____.

to   too

(tl)Blend Images/Alamy; (tr)Lars A. Niki/McGraw-Hill Education; (bl)moodboard/SuperStock; (br)Purestock/Getty Images

COLLABORATE

❶ Talk About It

Look at the picture. Read the title. Discuss what you see. Use these words.

balls   juggling   girl

Write about what you see.

I see _____

_____ .

Why is the girl juggling?

The girl is _____

_____ .

What is a talent show?

A talent show is _____

_____ .

Take notes as you read the story.

THE Talent Show

Essential Question

? **How do your actions affect others?**

Read about how Tina's actions affect Maura.

I shouted to my best friend. "Tina, there is a school talent show in three weeks!" My brother was teaching me how to **juggle**. I knew he could help me with my act.

Tina read the poster for the show. Tina said, "Maura, what is our act going to be?"

I said, "Our act? You want to do an act with me?" My hands squeezed my books tightly.

"Maura, it will be fun," Tina said.

I stopped for a minute before **continuing** to talk. "I have an idea …"

But Tina **interrupted** me. She said, "We can talk at lunch."

I wanted to do my own act, but I did not want to tell Tina. She is my best friend. But Tina always tells me what to do, and that is a problem. She always decides. This makes me feel bad.

I wanted to win the talent show. And I wanted to win on my own.

Chris Vallo

1 Specific Vocabulary A C T

Reread the first paragraph. The word *juggle* means "to toss and catch many balls at one time." Draw a box around the word that tells who is teaching Maura how to juggle.

2 Sentence Structure A C T

Reread the third paragraph. Circle the punctuation marks that show you someone is speaking. Who is speaking?

_____ is speaking.

COLLABORATE

3 Talk About It

Reread the seventh paragraph. What is Maura's problem?

Maura's problem is _____

_____.

21

Text Evidence

1 Sentence Structure A C T

Reread the first paragraph. In the second sentence, circle the word that connects the two things Tina has planned. Then complete the sentence.

Tina has planned to _____

_____.

2 Talk About It

Reread the third paragraph. Why does Tina not like Maura's idea? Circle the sentences that tell you.

Tina does not like Maura's idea

because _____

_____.

3 Specific Vocabulary A C T

Reread the sixth paragraph. The word *respect* means "showing you care about a person's ideas and feelings." Underline the person who does not respect Maura.

At lunch, Tina said, "I have planned our act. We will sing a song and do a dance routine."

I said, "I have an idea, too." I told her about my juggling act.

Tina thought about it. Then she said, "No, I don't think I can learn to juggle. I will probably drop all the balls. We do not want to be humiliated."

I was very unhappy. So I ran around the track two times.

My grandmother picked me up after school, and I explained my problem to her.

My grandmother listened carefully. "Tina does not **respect** your idea. But you do not think your idea is important."

I did not understand.

My grandmother explained, "You cannot always do what your friends want. You are responsible for your own actions."

I asked my grandmother for help.

She said, "Tell the truth. Tina needs to know what you want. And telling the truth is good for your "self-esteem."

At home, I called Tina. I told her I was going to do my juggling act. Tina was not friendly on the phone, and I was worried that she was mad at me.

The next day, Tina described her act and her costume for the show. But the big surprise came at recess.

Tina asked, "What game do you want to play?"

I think standing up for myself and telling Tina how I felt was the best thing to do.

Make Connections

? Talk about how Maura was affected by Tina's actions. **ESSENTIAL QUESTION**

Tell about a time when someone did not listen to your ideas. What did you do? **TEXT TO SELF**

Chris Vallo

Text Evidence

1 Comprehension

Problem and Solution

Reread the third paragraph. How does Maura solve her problem? Underline the sentence that tells you.

2 Sentence Structure **A C T**

Reread the third sentence in the third paragraph. Circle the word that connects the two parts of the sentence. Underline the part of the sentence that tells why Maura was worried.

COLLABORATE

3 Talk About It

Reread the fourth and fifth paragraphs. Why was Maura surprised that Tina wanted to play a game?

Maura was surprised Tina wanted to play a game because

_____

_____

Respond to the Text

Partner Discussion Work with a partner. Read the questions about "The Talent Show." Show where you found text evidence. Write the page numbers. Then describe what you learned.

What did you learn about Tina and Maura?

I read that Tina and Maura are _____.

For the talent show, Maura wants to _____.

For the talent show, Tina wants to _____.

Text Evidence 🔍

Page(s): _____

Page(s): _____

Page(s): _____

What problem does Maura have?

I read that Tina always tells Maura _____.

In the text, Maura's grandmother tells Maura to _____.

Maura tells Tina that _____.

Text Evidence 🔍

Page(s): _____

Page(s): _____

Page(s): _____

Group Discussion Present your answers to the group. Cite text evidence for your ideas. Listen to and discuss the group's opinions about your ideas.

I think your idea is _____.

Write Work with a partner. Look at your notes about "The Talent Show." Write your answer to the essential question. Use text evidence to support your answer. Use vocabulary words in your writing.

How do Tina's actions affect Maura?

In the beginning of the story, Tina does not let Maura _____

_____

_____.

Maura solves her problem with Tina by _____

_____

_____.

At the end of the story, Maura feels better because Tina _____

_____.

Share Writing Present your writing to the class. Discuss their opinions. Think about their ideas. Explain why you agree or disagree with their ideas. You can say:

I agree with _____.

I do not agree because _____.

Petra

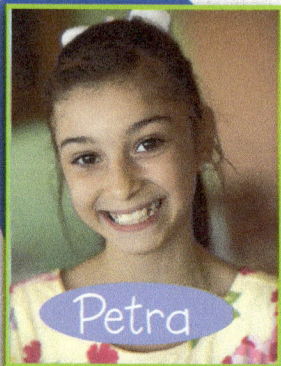

Take Notes About the Text I took notes on the chart about what Maura and Tina say to each other about the talent show. This will help me answer the question: *What did Maura and Tina say to each other on the phone at the end of the story? Use details from the story.*

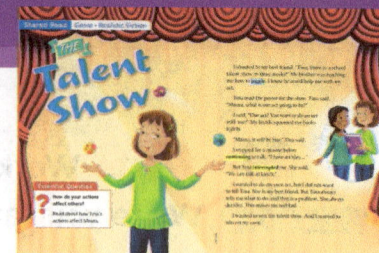

pages 20–23

Maura	Tina
Maura tells Tina about the talent show.	Tina wants to do an act with Maura.
Maura wants to juggle.	Tina wants to sing and dance.
Maura calls Tina. She tells her she wants to juggle.	Tina was not friendly.

Write About the Text I used my notes from the chart to write about what I think Maura and Tina said to each other on the phone.

Student Model: *Narrative Text*

"Hi, Tina. It's Maura, I have to talk to you about the talent show."

"I picked a song. I want to show you a dance move, too. Can you practice tomorrow?" Tina said.

"No, Tina," I said. "I'm going to do my own act. I'm going to juggle."

"What about our act?" Tina said.

"You can do the act on your own," I said.

"Oh, okay. I'll see you in school," Tina said.

TALK ABOUT IT

COLLABORATE

Text Evidence

Draw a box around a detail that comes from the notes. Does the dialogue support the detail?

Grammar

Circle the pronoun in "I picked a song." Who does *I* refer to?

Connect Ideas

Underline the first two sentences in the second paragraph. How can you use the word *and* to connect the sentences?

Your Turn

COLLABORATE

Write what Maura and Tina say to each other when Maura chooses a game to play. Use details from the story.

>> Go Digital
Write your response online. Use your editing checklist.

27

? **Essential Question**
How do people respond to natural disasters?

>> *Go Digital*

What do you see in the photograph? Describe what the helicopter is doing. Write words in the chart. Discuss how people help others.

Helping Others

Discuss how people help with a forest fire. Use the words from the chart. You can say:

During a forest fire, people _____.

They also _____.

More Vocabulary

COLLABORATE

Look at the picture and read the word. Then read the sentences.
Talk about the word with a partner. Answer the question. Write your own sentence.

surface

There is food on the **surface** of the table.

What word means *surface*?

top   **beside**   **under**

What is on the surface of your desk?

_____ is on the *surface* of my desk.

warn

The weatherman can **warn** us about the weather.

What word means *warn*?

ask   **tell**   **see**

What can you warn someone about?

I *warn* someone about _____.

Words and Phrases: Compound Words

A compound word is made up of two words.

land + form = landform

A mountain is a **landform**.

land + slide = landslide

Rain can cause a **landslide**.

COLLABORATE **Talk with a partner. Look at the pictures. Read the sentences. Circle the compound word that completes the sentence.**

A hill is a _____.

landslide   landform

A _____ causes rocks to fall.

landform   landslide

COLLABORATE

1 Talk About It

Look at the photograph. Read the title. Discuss what you see. Use these words.

change Grand Canyon landform

Write about what you see

I see _____

_____.

What are the people doing?

The people are _____

_____.

Describe the landform.

The landform looks _____

_____.

Take notes as you read the text.

A World of CHANGE

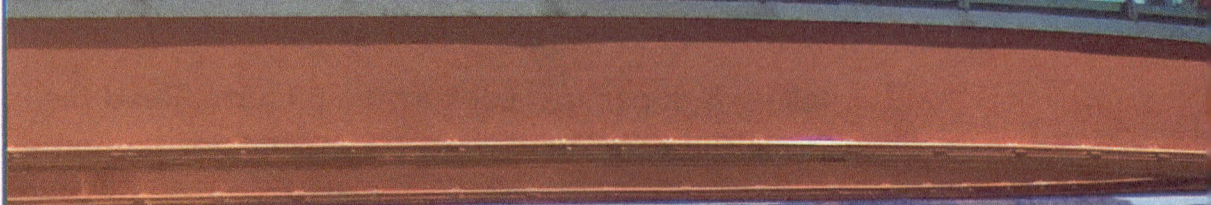

Essential Question

? **How do people respond to natural disasters?**

Read about how people prepare for natural disasters.

The Grand Canyon Skywalk, Arizona

E arth changes every day. Nature changes the ==surface== of Earth all the time. Some changes are slow. Some changes are fast. Both natural changes have a great effect on Earth.

Slow Changes

Weathering, erosion, and deposition are slow **natural processes**. They take many years to change the surface of Earth.

Weathering happens when rain, snow, sun, and wind break rocks into small pieces. The small pieces of rock turn into soil.

Erosion happens when the pieces of rock and soil are moved to other places. They are moved by the wind or water. Erosion causes landforms, such as mountains, to get smaller. The Grand Canyon is an example of erosion. It was carved by a river. The erosion took thousands of years.

Deposition happens when soil and rocks are put in new places. Water can move a lot of soil and rocks to one place. This deposition can form a beach. But it takes a long time.

Text Evidence

1 Specific Vocabulary A C T

Reread the first sentence in the second paragraph. The words *natural processes* mean "things that happen in nature that cause changes." Underline the three slow natural processes.

2 Comprehension
Compare and Contrast

Reread the second paragraph. How are weathering, erosion, and deposition alike?

_____, _____, and _____

are alike because they all _____

_____.

3 Sentence Structure A C T

Reread the third sentence in the fourth paragraph. Circle the commas that break the sentence into parts. What is an example of a landform?

An example of a landform is a

_____.

1 Sentence Structure (A)(C)(T)

Reread the first sentence in the first paragraph. What noun does the pronoun *it* refer to? Write the noun and pronoun.

_____

2 Comprehension

Compare and Contrast

Reread the second and third paragraphs. How are fast natural processes different than slow natural processes?

Fast processes are different than slow natural processes because

_____

_____.

3 Specific Vocabulary (A)(C)(T)

Reread the third paragraph. Look at the words *volcanic eruption*. Draw a box around the words that tell what a volcanic eruption is.

Erosion is a slow process but it can cause big problems. Ocean waves can destroy a beach. Sometimes people try to stop beach erosion. They build walls to block waves. They also put in plants. The plant roots hold the soil in place.

Fast Changes

Some natural processes happen very fast. Volcanic eruptions and landslides make fast changes. They can be powerful and cause a lot of destruction. This is why they are called natural disasters.

A volcanic eruption can happen with no warning. A volcano is formed around an opening in the crust of Earth. A **volcanic eruption** happens when hot melted rock is pushed up. The melted rock flows out of the volcano.

Like volcanic eruptions, landslides happen very fast. There is no warning. Many times landslides happen when there is a lot of rain. The rain **loosens** rocks and soil on hills or mountains. This causes rocks and soil to slide down a hill very quickly.

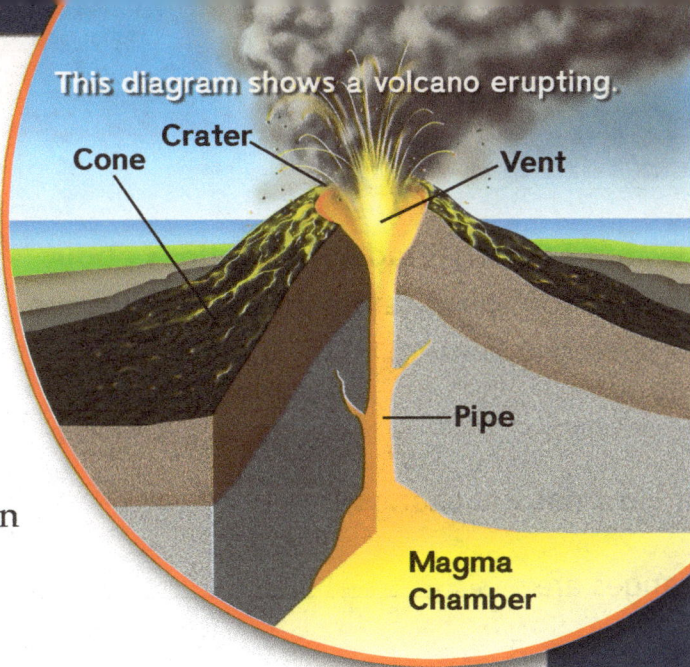

This diagram shows a volcano erupting.

Cone

Crater

Vent

Pipe

Magma Chamber

Be Prepared

People can prevent the effects of slow changes. But they cannot prevent the effects of fast changes. So scientists try to predict when landslides and volcanic eruptions will happen. Then they can **warn** people. But they are difficult to predict. So it is important for communities to have an emergency plan. This will help save lives.

Natural processes change the surface of Earth. But those changes make Earth an amazing planet!

Make Connections

? Talk about different ways that people prepare for natural disasters. ESSENTIAL QUESTION

How can you help others who have been in a natural disaster? TEXT TO SELF

1 Comprehension
Compare and Contrast

Reread the first paragraph. How is a landslide like a volcanic eruption? Circle the words that tell you.

2 Specific Vocabulary A C T

Reread the first paragraph. The word *loosens* means "to make something less tight." Underline what a lot of rain loosens. Circle what happens when rain loosens rocks and soil on hills.

COLLABORATE

3 Talk About It

Why is it important for communities to be prepared for natural disasters?

It is important to be prepared

because _____

_____.

(bkgd) Westend61/Getty Images; (r) Neil Stewart

Respond to the Text

Partner Discussion Work with a partner. Read the questions about "A World of Change." Show where you found text evidence. Write the page numbers. Then describe what you learned.

COLLABORATE

What did you learn about slow natural changes?

I read that slow natural changes are _____ ,

_____ , and _____ .

In the text, slow natural processes happen over _____ .

Erosion can cause big problems like _____ .

Text Evidence 🔍

Page(s): _____

Page(s): _____

Page(s): _____

What did you learn about fast natural changes?

I learned volcanic eruptions can happen _____ .

I learned landslides happen _____ .

Emergency plans are important because _____ .

Text Evidence 🔍

Page(s): _____

Page(s): _____

Page(s): _____

COLLABORATE

Group Discussion Present your answers to the group. Cite text evidence for your ideas. Listen to and discuss the group's opinions about your ideas.

I think your idea is _____ .

Write Work with a partner. Look at your notes about "A World of Change." Then write your answer to the essential question. Use text evidence to support your answer. Use vocabulary words in your writing.

How do people prepare for natural disasters?

People can stop beach erosion by _____

_____

_____.

People cannot prevent volcanic eruptions and landslides so scientists try

to _____

_____.

According to the author, it is important for communities to have _____

_____.

Share Writing Present your writing to the class. Then talk about their opinions. Think about their ideas. Explain why you agree or disagree with their ideas. You can say:

I agree with _____.

I do not agree because _____.

Write to Sources

Take Notes About the Text I took notes on this chart to answer the question: *How does the author help us understand fast and slow changes to the surface of Earth? Use text evidence.*

Sara

Different: Slow Changes

Alike: Slow and Fast Changes

Different: Fast Changes

Changes take a long time. People try to protect land from slow changes.

Changes the surface of Earth.

Changes happen suddenly. People cannot stop.

Thinkstock Images/Stockbyte/Getty Images

Write About the Text I used notes from my chart to write
a paragraph about slow and fast changes to Earth's surface.

Student Model: *Informational Text*

The author writes about slow and fast
changes to Earth. Both can change the surface
of Earth. One kind of slow change is called
erosion. Another kind is weathering. They take
a long time to happen. People try to protect
the land from these changes. But fast changes
happen very fast. They are changes like
landslides and volcanoes. People cannot protect
the land when they happen. Slow and fast
changes are alike and different.

TALK ABOUT IT

COLLABORATE

Text Evidence
Draw a box around a sentence that names a
kind of slow change. What is the other kind of
slow change in the text?

Grammar
Circle a present-tense verb. Why did Sara use
the present tense?

Condense Ideas
Underline the two sentences that tell about fast
changes. How can you condense the sentences
into one detailed sentence?

Your Turn
COLLABORATE

What kind of change does the
volcano diagram show? Give a detail.
Use text evidence.

>> *Go Digital*
Write your response online. Use your editing checklist.

39

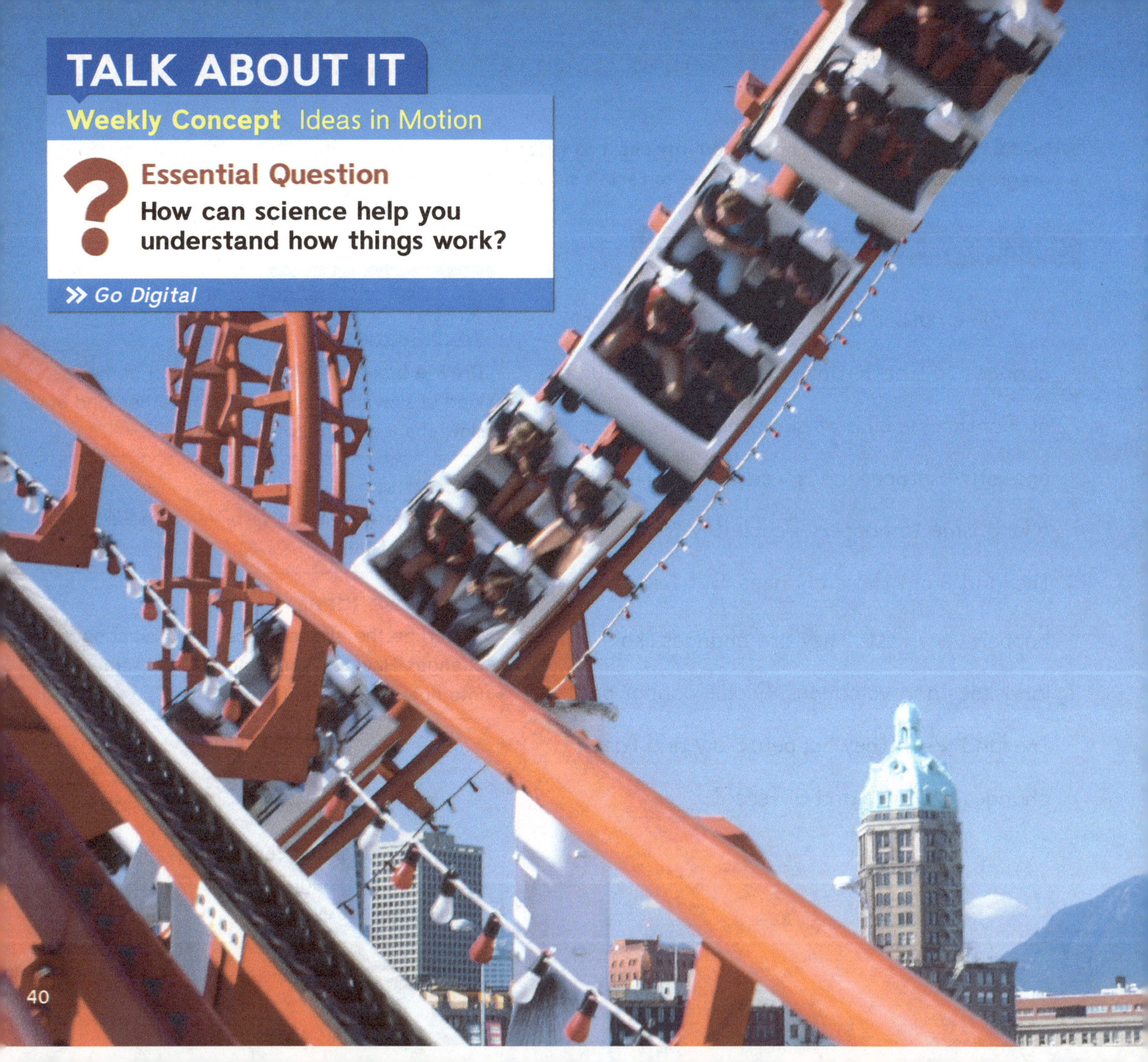

? Essential Question

How can science help you understand how things work?

>> *Go Digital*

COLLABORATE **How is the roller coaster moving? Write the words in the chart.**
Discuss how science can help you understand how machines work.

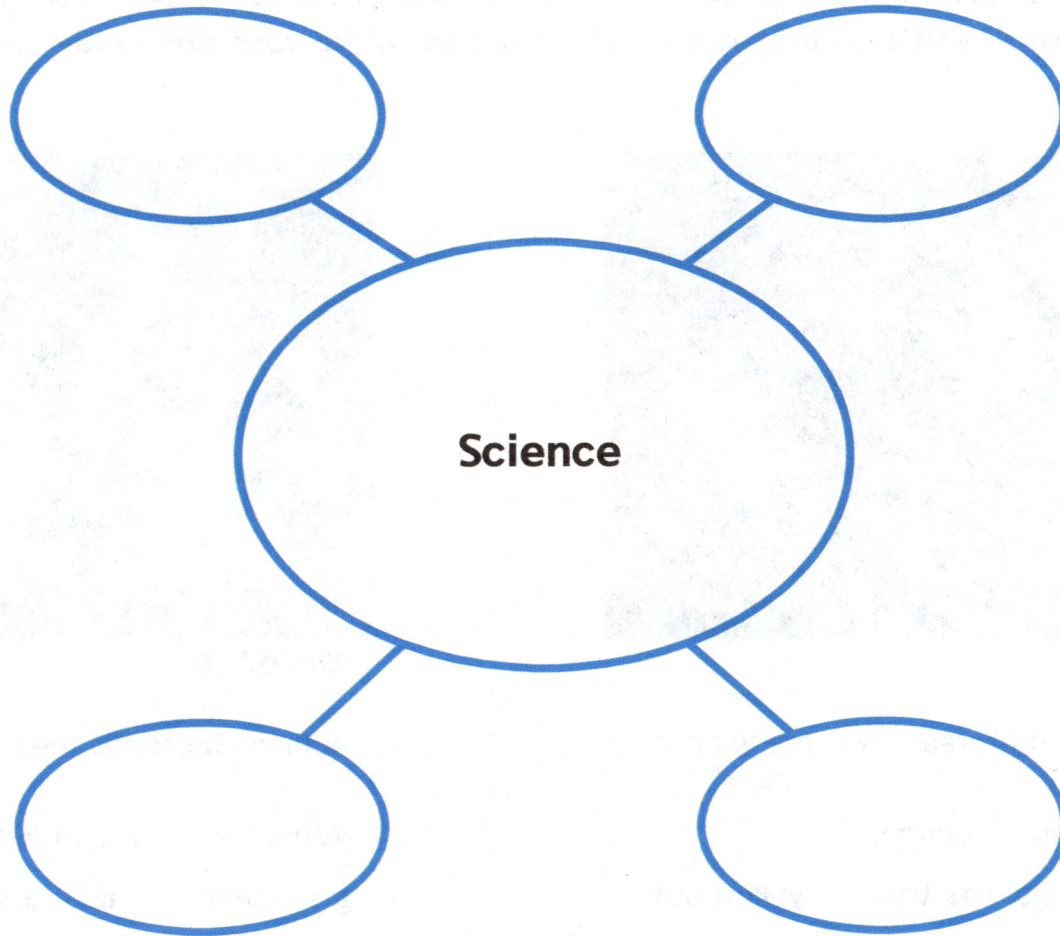

Science

Discuss how science can help you understand how the roller coaster works. Use the words from the chart. You can say:

Science can help me understand how the roller coaster moves

_____.

Gunter Marx/Alamy Stock Photo

41

More Vocabulary

Look at the picture and read the word. Then read the sentences. Talk about the word with a partner. Answer the question. Write your own sentence.

claimed

The boy **claimed** his team was the winner.

Which words mean *claimed*?

ran away   said was true   yelled out

Have you ever claimed something?

I claimed _____.

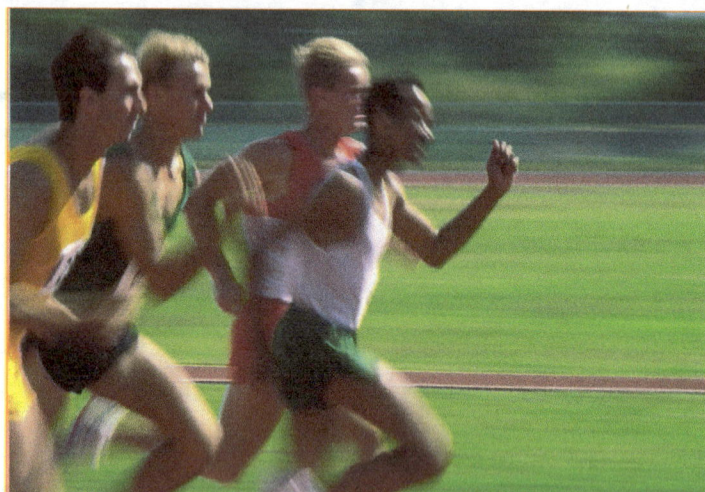

increase

Runners **increase** their speed in a race.

Which words mean *increase*?

go slower   make a stop   go faster

When do you increase your speed?

I increase my speed when _____.

Words and Phrases: Comparative Endings *–er* and *–est*

The ending *–er* is used to compare two things.

I am big.

My dad is **bigger** than me.

The ending *–est* is used to compare three or more things.

Sarah is fast.

Jake is the **fastest** in our class.

COLLABORATE **Talk with a partner. Look at the pictures. Read the sentences. Write the word that completes the sentence.**

The hill is the _____ in town.

steeper   steepest

My mom is _____ than me.

taller   tallest

COLLABORATE

1 Talk About It

Look at the picture. Read the title. Discuss what you see. Use these words.

race boys woman skates

Write about what you see.

I see _____

_____.

Who are the people you see?

The people are _____

_____.

What is the woman doing?

The woman is _____

_____.

Take notes as you read.

THE BIG Race

This virtual race car is cool.

Let's try it!

Essential Question

?

How can science help you understand how things work?

Read how Alex and Liam want to use science to help them win a race.

44

Speech bubble: I'm Clara. Welcome!

Alex and Liam wanted to build a car for a race. So, they went to the science museum. They wanted to learn how to build a fast car. A woman named Clara was there to help.

"Hi, I'm Clara. Are you the boys who want to know what will make a car go fast?"

"Yes, I'm Alex, and that's Liam," Alex said.

"Why are you wearing skates, Clara?" Liam asked.

"I'm a champion skater! The skates let me get around faster," Clara claimed. "And I'm a scientist, too," she said. "Follow me!"

IT'S ABOUT SPEED

"Welcome to our exhibit," Clara said as they entered a large room. "Tell me about the race."

"There will be 20 cars. We'll be going down the steepest hill in town!" Alex said.

"Sounds exciting! It must be exciting to go fast!" Clara said. Then she pressed buttons on a machine. "This is a virtual race car. This screen shows you the race course and your speed. Speed is how far an object moves in a certain amount of time."

Craig Phillips

1 Sentence Structure A C T

Reread the first paragraph. Underline the people that the pronoun *They* refers to. Circle the words that tell what they wanted. Rewrite the third sentence with the names of the people.

_____ wanted

to learn how to build a fast car.

2 Specific Vocabulary A C T

Reread the sixth paragraph. The word *exhibit* means "a show, display, or presentation." Circle the words that tell you where the exhibit is. Reread the eighth paragraph. What is in the exhibit? Underline the words.

3 Comprehension

Reread the last paragraph. Underline the word that tells you how far an object moves in a certain amount of time.

Text Evidence

1 Sentence Structure A C T

Reread the first sentence in the first paragraph. Underline the subject that tells who the sentence is about. Circle the words that tell what the subject is doing.

2 Specific Vocabulary A C T

Reread the second paragraph. *Motion* means "movement." What affects motion? Draw a box around the word that tells you.

3 Comprehension
Cause and Effect

Reread the fourth paragraph. Circle the word that tells what causes things to move. Underline what will cause something to move faster if two things are the same size.

FORCES AT WORK

Clara pointed to the car. Clara said the boys could use it to practice for the race.

Clara said, "Since you want to build a fast car, you need to know about forces and how they affect **motion**."

"What's a force?" asked Liam.

Clara told the boys that a force is a push or a pull. Forces cause things to move. She said, "When I apply a big enough force on an object, like this stool, it moves." She then explained that if two things are the same size, the one that gets the bigger push will move faster.

Alex guessed that a big push at the top of the hill would **increase** the speed of their car. Clara told him he was right.

A force is a push or a pull.

There's a sharp curve coming up!

The car will speed up now!

GRAVITY AND FRICTION

Then Clara told the boys about gravity. "Gravity is a pulling force between two objects," she explained. "Gravity is the force that will pull your car down the hill."

"How do we stop?" Liam asked.

Clara explained, "Friction is a force between two surfaces. It slows or stops objects from moving." She showed the boys how the friction between the rubber stoppers on her skates and the floor slowed her down.

Alex and Liam thanked Clara. Now they knew the science behind winning a race.

You need friction.

Make Connections

? Talk about ways that science can help you understand how objects move. **ESSENTIAL QUESTION**

How can science help you understand your favorite activities? **TEXT TO SELF**

Craig Phillips

1 Comprehension
Cause and Effect

Reread the first paragraph. What will cause the car to move down the hill? Circle the word that tells you.

2 Sentence Structure **A C T**

Reread the second sentence in the third paragraph. Circle the noun in the first sentence that can replace the pronoun *It*.

COLLABORATE
3 Talk About It

Talk about the things Alex and Liam learned at the museum that will help them in the race. Then write about it.

Alex and Liam learned about _____

_____.

They can use this information to

_____

_____.

47

Respond to the Text

Partner Discussion Work with a partner. Read the questions about "The Big Race." Show where you found text evidence. Write the page numbers. Then discuss what you learned.

What did you learn about forces?

A force is a _____.   Page(s): _____

Forces cause things to _____.   Page(s): _____

When an object is pushed, _____.   Page(s): _____

Text Evidence

What did you learn about gravity and friction?

Gravity is a force that _____.   Page(s): _____

Friction is a force that _____.   Page(s): _____

Text Evidence

Group Discussion Present your answers to the group. Cite text evidence for your ideas. Listen to and discuss the group's opinions about your ideas.

I think your idea is _____.

Write Work with a partner. Look at your notes about "The Big Race." Write your answer to the essential question. Use text evidence to support your answer. Use vocabulary words in your writing.

How can science help Alex and Liam win a soap box derby race?

A car that gets a big push at the top of a hill will _____

_____

_____.

Gravity will pull the car _____

_____

_____.

Friction will help to _____

_____.

Share Writing Present your writing to the class. Then talk about their opinions. Think about their ideas. Explain why you agree or disagree with their ideas. You can say:

I agree with _____.

I do not agree because _____.

49

Write to Sources

Henry

Take Notes About the Text I took notes on the idea web to answer the question: *What does the author tell about how forces affect motion?*

The author tells about how forces affect motion.

Pushes and pulls are forces that move things.

Gravity is a pulling force.

Friction is a force that slows or stops a motion.

Comstock/Stockbyte/Getty Images

Write About the Text I used notes from my idea web to write a paragraph about how the author describes forces.

The author tells about different forces. Pushes and pulls will move things. Gravity is a force that pulls things down. Friction is a force that slows down things. Friction stops things from moving, too. The author shows how forces affect motion.

TALK ABOUT IT

COLLABORATE

Text Evidence

Draw a box around a detail from the notes that tells what a push or a pull does. Why did Henry include this detail?

Grammar

Circle the words that describe *friction*. Why did Henry add these words?

Connecting Ideas

Underline the sentences that tell what friction is. How can you connect these sentences using the word *and?*

Your Turn

COLLABORATE

What does the author tell about gravity? Use text evidence.

>> *Go Digital*
Write your response online. Use your editing checklist.

? Essential Question

How can starting a business help others?

>> *Go Digital*

COLLABORATE What is the woman doing? Describe how a business can help others. Write words in the chart.

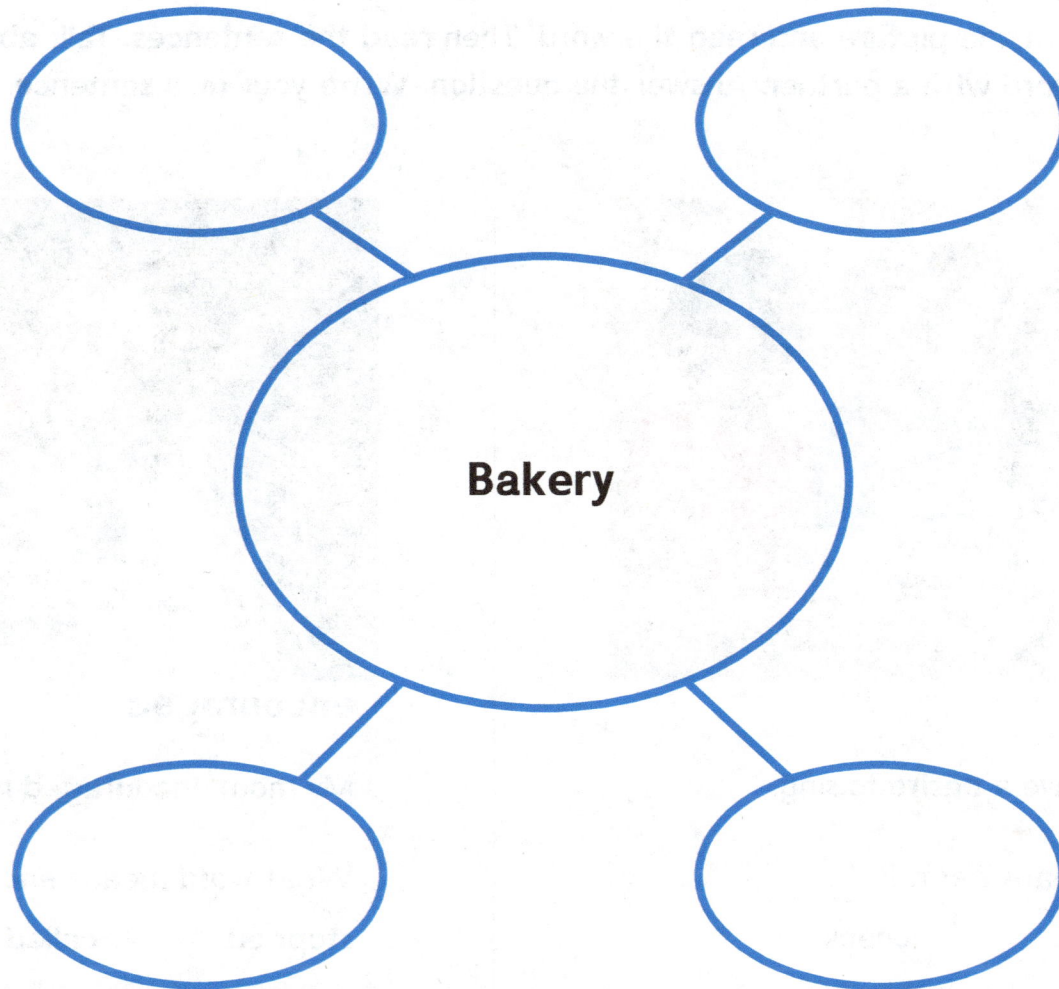

Bakery

Discuss how a business can help others. Use the words from the chart. You can say:

A business helps _____. It also _____.

More Vocabulary

Look at the picture and read the word. Then read the sentences. Talk about the word with a partner. Answer the question. Write your own sentence.

desire

The children have a **desire** to sing.

What word means *desire*?

last   wish   check

What do you have a desire to do?

I have a desire to _____.

encouraged

My mom **encouraged** me to keep trying.

What word means *encouraged*?

stopped   called   helped

What have you been encouraged to do?

I have been encouraged to _____.

Words and Phrases: Possessive Pronouns

The word *his* tells about what Jake owns.

The cat belongs to Jake.

Jake plays with his cat.

The word *their* tells about what the family owns.

The dog belongs to the family.

The family takes their dog for a walk.

COLLABORATE **Talk with a partner. Look at the pictures. Read the sentences. Write the possessive pronoun that completes the sentence.**

The horse is eating _____ hay.

their   his

The children eat _____ lunch.

his   their

(tl)PhotoAlto/SuperStock; (tr)Juice Images/SuperStock; (bl)goce risteski/iStock/360/Getty Images; (br)Ken Karp/McGraw-Hill Education

COLLABORATE

① Talk About It

Look at the photograph. Read the title. Discuss what you see. Use these words.

shoes   children   man

I see _____

_____

_____.

Who are the people you see?

The people are _____

_____.

What is the man doing?

The man is _____

_____

Take notes as you read.

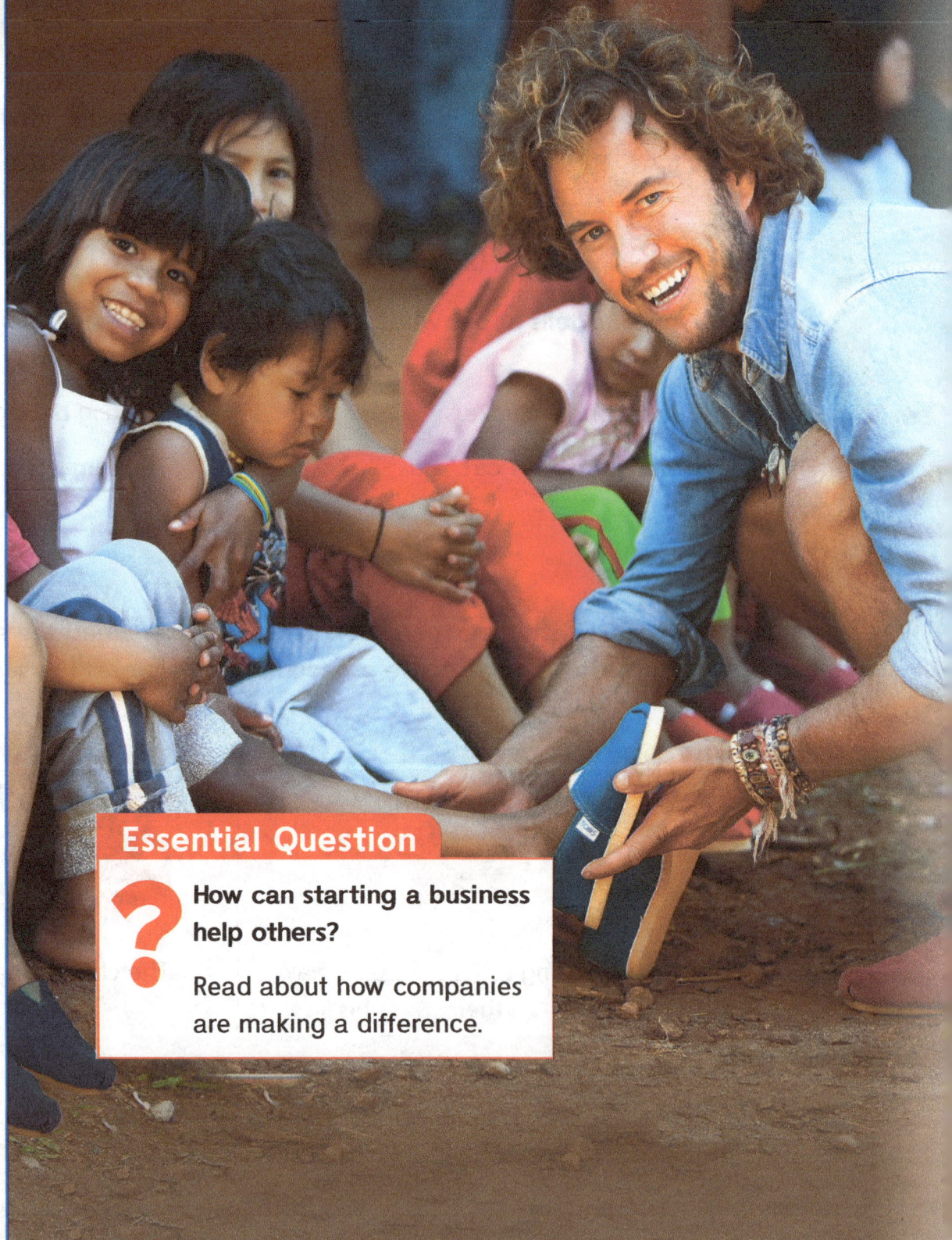

Essential Question

? **How can starting a business help others?**

Read about how companies are making a difference.

Dollars and $ENSE

These businesses are successful in helping others.

Good business is not always about making the most money. A business can have success in other ways. Many large companies are trying to help people in need.

A Different Business

Blake Mycoskie had four businesses. But he wanted to do something different from his usual work routine. So in 2006, he traveled to Argentina, South America. He visited poor villages where very few children had shoes.

Mycoskie had a desire to help. He said, "I'm going to start a shoe company. For every pair I sell, I am going to give one pair to a kid in need."

Mycoskie used his own money to start the business. He named the company TOMS: Shoes for Tomorrow. The shoes look like the shoes Argentine workers wear.

TOMS gives away one pair of shoes for every pair that is sold. By 2011, TOMS had donated over one million pairs of shoes.

1 Sentence Structure A C T

Reread the third sentence in the second paragraph. Circle the commas.

What does the first part of the sentence tell? _____

What does the second part of the sentence tell? _____

2 Comprehension

Main Idea and Key Details

Reread the third paragraph. The main idea is that Mycoskie had a desire to help. Underline a key detail that tells about the main idea.

3 Specific Vocabulary A C T

Reread the last paragraph. The word *donated* means "gave something to someone or an organization to help them." Circle the words that tell you what Mycoskie donated.

Text Evidence

① Specific Vocabulary (ACT)

Reread the second paragraph. The word *charity* means "an organization that gives money or things to people in need." Underline what the company gave to charity.

② Sentence Structure (ACT)

Reread the fourth sentence in the second paragraph. Underline the noun in the paragraph that the pronoun *it* refers to. Circle the things it does.

③ Comprehension

Main Idea and Key Details

Reread the third paragraph. The main idea is that the company raises money by selling T-shirts. Write a key detail that tells about the main idea.

_____

_____

_____.

TOMS' employees unpack shoes to give away.

The company now sells eyeglasses. One pair of eyeglasses is donated to a person in need for every pair that is sold.

Giving Back

Have you ever seen a Hard Rock Cafe? The company owns restaurants and hotels. In 1990, the company started a new enterprise. It raises money and gives it to **charity**. Since then, the company has given millions of dollars to charity.

One way the company raises money is by selling T-shirts. Rock musicians design the art for the T-shirts. Then the shirts are sold on the Internet. Part of the money is given to charity.

The people who work at the company are **encouraged** to raise money for their community, too. Every store does it differently.

The Hard Rock Cafes are successful and give back to the community.

Top Five Biggest Charities

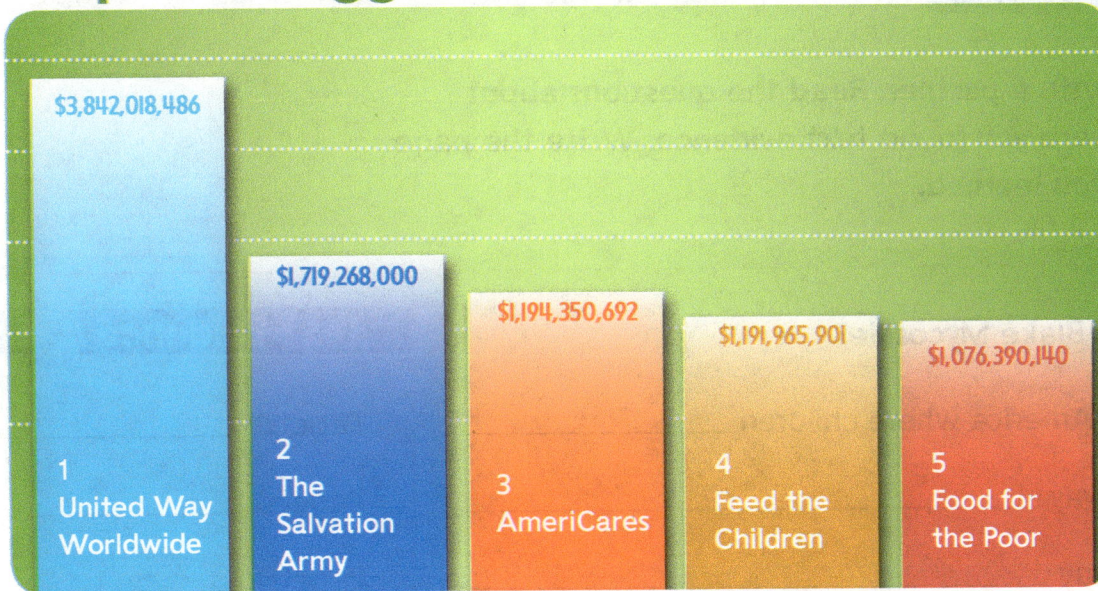

Source: The Chronicle Of Philanthropy

Rank	Charity	Amount
1	United Way Worldwide	$3,842,018,486
2	The Salvation Army	$1,719,268,000
3	AmeriCares	$1,194,350,692
4	Feed the Children	$1,191,965,901
5	Food for the Poor	$1,076,390,140

Individuals and businesses are helping people in need. This graph shows the American charities that got the most donations in one recent year. It shows how much money they raised.

The restaurant workers in Hollywood, Florida, worked with high school students. They did an event to raise money for the Make-A-Wish Foundation. The foundation fills the wishes of children who are very sick.

Helping Others

Every day companies are thinking of new ways to help people in need. Making money is important for companies.

However, helping others is just as important. Helping others is good business!

Make Connections

? How do the companies in this article help others?
ESSENTIAL QUESTION

If you owned a business, how would you use some of your money to help others? **TEXT TO SELF**

Text Evidence

1 Comprehension
Main Idea and Key Details

Reread the first paragraph. Circle a key detail about the Make-A-Wish Foundation.

2 Sentence Structure A C T

Reread the first sentence in the last paragraph. *Companies* is the subject of the sentence. Underline the words that tell what the subject is doing.

COLLABORATE

3 Talk About It

Describe how a business can help others.

A company can help others by

_____

_____

_____

Respond to the Text

Partner Discussion Work with a partner. Read the questions about "Dollars and Sense." Show where you found text evidence. Write the page numbers. Then discuss what you learned.

What did you learn about Blake Mycoskie?

Text Evidence 🔍

He visited villages in South America where children _____. Page(s): _____

He started TOMS to give away _____. Page(s): _____

The company also gives away _____. Page(s): _____

What did you learn about the Hard Rock Cafe?

Text Evidence 🔍

I read that it raises money by _____. Page(s): _____

People who work for the company are encouraged to _____. Page(s): _____

One store raises money for a charity that helps _____. Page(s): _____

Group Discussion Present your answers to the group. Cite text evidence for your ideas. Listen to and discuss the group's opinions about your ideas.

I think your idea is _____.

Write Work with a partner. Look at your notes about "Dollars and Sense." Write your answer to the Essential Question. Use text evidence to support your answer. Use vocabulary words in your writing.

COLLABORATE

> **How can a business help others?**
>
> A business can help others by giving _____
>
> _____ .
>
> A business can help raise money to _____
>
> _____ .
>
> A company can encourage their workers to _____ .

Share Writing Present your writing to the class. Then talk about their opinions. Think about their ideas. Explain why you agree or disagree with their ideas. You can say:

COLLABORATE

I agree with _____ .

I do not agree because _____ .

Write to Sources

Kendall

Take Notes About the Text I took notes on the idea web to answer the question: *Do you think TOMS does a good job of helping people?*

pages 56–59

Dollars and $ENSE

These businesses are successful in helping others.

Opinion
TOMS does a good job of helping people.

TOMS gives away shoes to kids in need.

TOMS gives away one pair of shoes for every pair they sell.

Now they donate eyeglasses, too.

Write About the Text I used notes from my idea web to write an opinion about TOMS and how it helps people.

I think TOMS does a good job of helping people. TOMS gives shoes to kids in need. They give away one pair of shoes for every pair they sell. They give away eyeglasses, too. TOMS sells things and gives things away. Everyone wins!

TALK ABOUT IT

COLLABORATE

Text Evidence

Draw a box around a detail that comes from the notes. Does the sentence provide a supporting detail?

Grammar

Underline the words that describe the kids. Why did the writer add these words?

Connect Ideas

Circle the sentence that tells another thing TOMS gives away. How can you use the word *and* to connect the sentences?

Your Turn

COLLABORATE

What other company is good at helping people? Use text evidence.

>> *Go Digital*
Write your response online. Use your editing checklist.